Cracked, Not Broken

Kayla Allen

BookLeaf
Publishing

India | USA | UK

Presentation by *BookLeaf Publishing*

Web: www.bookleafpub.com

E-mail: info@bookleafpub.com

ISBN: 9789363311640

First edition 2024

PREFACE

Some of these poems may have dark themes or
be difficult to read.

Life

I want a house full of laughter
For the rest of my days
I want someone to see me
And not run away
I want a house full of music
Where I'm free to sing
I want to come home
And feel at peace
I want a house full of love
Most important of all
I want a house full of laughter
Over nothing at all

I want a life full of joy
And a heart full of smiles
I want a life full of love
And books stacked up in piles
I want a life full of peace
And the rest that I crave
I want to love someone
Who feels the same
I want a life full of laughter
That's all that I ask
To be happy for real
Not sad under the mask

I want a life full of laughter
I'll build it with my bare hands
I'll create a safe space
And a soft place to land
I'll care for the property
And I'll care for my heart
Because now is the time
My life finally starts

You

You're the sun to me
Filling my days with ecstasy
Supplying chlorophyll to my leaves
In your warmth I'm finally free

You're the sea to me
Your calming waves lull me to sleep
My broken soul has found its peace
Your heart holds my tranquility

You're the rain to me
Kissing my skin playfully
A drumbeat playing steadily
A song you wrote only for me

You're the stars to me
My sparkling infinity
Constellations shining brilliantly
Your soul shines so beautifully

You're a million things to me
My heart's missing puzzle piece
Your heart is all I'll ever need
You'll always be the sun to me

Reaper

I was asleep
Drowning in puddles 10 feet deep
The reaper cast his spell on me
Tempting me with sweet release
He sang his lullaby so sweet
And as I slept he smothered me

With an aching in my bones
I carefully approached his throne
Begging to once more see the light
With one more chance I'd do it right
But my soul was his eternal prize
He was deaf to all my cries

I am asleep
He as my soul and it's his to keep
He crossed his fingers silently
For every promise he made to me
So I am his and he is mine
Me and my reaper for all of time

If You Let Me

If you let me
I'll show you
Where darkness meets light
I'll take your hand
And show you
That it'll be alright

If you let me
I'll free you
From the prison of the past
I'll give you love
Like medicine
Until your heart is free at last

Asleep

In your chaos I fell asleep
Ambling aimlessly
Praying you wouldn't see
Me

Never in my wildest dreams
Did I see
You breaking every part of me
Shamelessly

You hurt me so easily
Curse my fragility
Rage complicated everything
Happily

In your chaos I lost me
I counted sheep
Pretending not to see
Purposefully

Home

I thought a home was four walls
Perhaps a piece of land
But now I know it's anywhere
As long as we're holding hands
I thought I had to pay a price
Through mortgages or rent
But with you there beside me
I'd be happy in a tent
I thought home was a place
It turns out I was wrong
Home is where your heart is
And mine was with you all along

Maybe

Maybe all that happened
Was that it wasn't meant to be
When the sun would shine on you
Darkness would smother me
And when the sun would bathe me
In her effervescent light
You'd be lost inside the darkness
Stuck in eternal night
When my heart broke into pieces
You stepped over the glass
And when your heart would shatter
I too would walk right past
There was no intent to harm
Not a mean thought in our heads
But maybe some people just aren't destined
To be in each other's beds
Maybe all that happened
Was we got lost along the way
And even though I loved you once
It would only hurt to stay

Aching

The ache settles in my bones
Creaking like an old house
The sound of your footsteps
Reverberates through the halls
Our laughter haunts my heart
Touching the bruises goodbye left
It traces broken promises
Like I used to trace your skin
When darkness wraps around me
I can still feel your lips
Pressed against the base of my neck
Bathing me in I love you
Now I reach for you in a sleepy haze
My cold craving your warmth
But all I touch is emptiness
And the ache that settles in my bones

Part of Me

Part of me will always wonder
If the door was too heavy
Or if you didn't even try
Part of me will always feel
Like that little girl who begged
And asked God why you didn't love her
Part of me will always break
When a child holds their mom's hand
Because why couldn't it have been me?
Part of me will always be
Waiting with my face against the window
Asking strangers when you'd be home
Part of me will always hurt
I could burn down cities with my rage
Until the world is reduced to ashes
Part of me will always love
The ones who gave me life and took it
Leaving me to wander and wonder forever
Part of me will always ache
For the child you took and twisted
While you were chasing down a high
And part of me will always wonder
Why my heart wasn't worth protecting
And why you didn't even try

I Love You

My heart beats erratically
Spelling "I love you" in cursive
I feel every letter
Being etched on its chambers
I reach out with a fingertip
And touch the smile you gave me
It dances across my lips
Doing a dainty pirouette
My head lays on your chest
Your breaths a steady metronome
Guiding me safely from the sea
Like a lighthouse on the shore
Your lips smile against mine
And butterflies erupt from slumber
The whisper in sync
Filling me with "I love you"
My mind is tossing and turning
Drowning in my sea of fear
Your lips press gently against my spine
And comfort blooms in me like roses
You've taken my aching
And removed it somehow
A surgeon with a scapel
You replace it with warmth
My skin is filled with fire

Like the anticipation before a kiss
My fingers dance across your body
Leaving traces of "I love you."

Cinderella Dreams

My Cinderella dreams
Died long ago
Burning to ashes
In my childhood home

My white knight
Isn't coming, I fear
For if he existed
He would've been here

My ballgown is dusty
The slippers shattered
Thrown against the wall
When I thought I mattered

Cinderella dreams
Will never be my reality
So I'll care for the castle
That never cared for me

If I Could

If I could take it all back
I'd wipe away every tear
I'd remove your sadness
You'd never feel fear

If I could turn back time
I'd take back my words
I'd kiss you goodbye instead
And minimize the hurt

If I could take it all back
I'd walk the other way
Tell you I just wasn't ready
So it wouldn't end that way

If I could turn back time
I'd make everything right
Regret is the blanket
That covers me at night

Reasons

15

Your smell on my skin
Your breath in my hair
You're the drug I can't stop taking
I feel you everywhere

Your kiss on my lips
Your hand holding mine
I found home in your heart
And peace in your mind

Your understanding smile
Your head on my chest
Making me smile
Is what you do best

Your easy compassion
Your confidence too
There are a million reasons
Why I love you

Untitled

There are things undefined
In the depth of my mind
Others see rainbows
But I'm colorblind
My heart is not hard to find
In a field full of mines
But it's yours to keep
If you look into my eyes
My soul is so kind
Happier than my mind
It's light grows dimmer
With the passing of time
Things will stay undefined
Darkness plays with my mind
Everyone's laughing
But I don't have the time

Doll

Beautiful doll upon a shelf
Made for others
Never caring for herself
A warm smile painted
On porcelain skin
You boost others higher
But when do you win?

Beautiful doll
WIth no self esteem
You can't even sleep
Since you gave up on your dreams
All day every day
You bring others joy
But at the end of the day
You're only a toy

Such a beautiful doll
Everyone longs for a touch
You sold your soul for love
But you love too much
Waiting for someone
To come play with you
Hoping that someday
They'll love you too

Beautiful doll
Collecting dust
You're a slave to love
A prisoner of lust
You look in the mirror
Fix your makeup and smile
Hoping someone will see
Past the painted on smile

The Meadow

One night I went walking
With nowhere to go
I found an old forgotten trail
And thought I'd try something unknown
The trail took me through a forest
Over bridges, over streams
Through a field of wildflowers
That was so serene
I could've stopped and rested there
But my mind wanted more
Surely there was more out there
I dreamt of salty golden shores
With each step I went further
Leaving the meadow far behind
With each moment it grew darker
But I saw sunshine in my mind
I got so lost in my dreaming
The trail had disappeared
It was dark and I'd forgotten
Just how I'd gotten here
Panicking I looked around
Searching for the trail
I dug my fingers in the soil
And began to cry and wail
Eventually my tears ran dry

And I laid down on the ground
The silence wrapped itself around me
So I didn't hear a sound
As I let sleep overtake me
Something crept out of the dark
The reaper came to claim me
And stop the beating of my heart
He raised his scythe above his head
And sliced my heart in two
He took me back to the sunny meadow
Where my soul waits for you

You'll Think of Me

You'll think of me
When you drive down the freeway
And the radio plays my song
You'll think of me
When the sunset paints the sky
And you remember the color of my blush
You'll think of me
When darkness holds you at midnight
And you're left alone with your thoughts
You'll think of me
When a tear rolls down your face
And all you need is a warm embrace
You'll think of me
When you see me shining
But it's no longer for you
You'll think of me
When the wind blows leaves around
And you remember how it moved through my
hair
You'll think of me
When you have a bad day
And need a soft place to land
You'll think of me
Perhaps even reach for my comfort
And find nothing but cold air

You'll think of me
When you celebrate a victory
And wish I was there clapping beside you
You'll think of me
You'll reach out to me and I'll be gone
Leaving you with just a memory
I don't make promises
But I promise you this
You'll think of me

Untitled

The caterpillars that laid so dormant
Deep inside the cavity of my chest
Have finally emerged from their cocoons
Fluttering their new wings excitedly
Every time I see you smile

Lonely

Lonely like a sunset
Sinking down behind the trees
Lonely like a hurricane
Swirling uncontrollably
Lonely like a fire
Scorching everything I touch
Lonely like a love song
That no one likes that much
Lonely like an earthquake
Shaking everyone around
Lonely like a ladybug
Crawling slowly on the ground
Lonely like a blade of grass
That misses the wind
Lonely like a wallflower
Who wants the song to end
Lonely like a roller coaster
With no one in line
Lonely like a pocket watch
That can't tell the time
Lonely like a metronome
Ticking away the hours
Lonely like a rainstorm
With no one dancing in the showers
Lonely like a hand grenade

Waiting to explode
Lonely like a highway
With not one car on the road
Lonely like a sunset
That everyone can see
Lonely like a mirror
With no one looking into me

Untitled

On the brink of collapse
About to relapse
My head's in the noose
It's no use
What's the point in trying
If I always lose?

Perfect

I never thought I'd see the day
When someone would find my heart
On the ground like a penny
And would stop and pick it up
Turning it over in their hands
Before putting it against their chest
Holding it gently and whispering
"It's perfect."

www.ingramcontent.com/pod-product-compliance
Lightning Source LLC
LaVergne TN
LVHW041253200726
843507LV00013B/2950